Sibilance

poems

Sibilance

SALLY VAN DOREN

LOUISIANA STATE UNIVERSITY PRESS | BATON ROUGE

Published by Louisiana State University Press
lsupress.org

LSU Press Paperback Original

DESIGNER: Michelle A. Neustrom
TYPEFACE: Calluna

COVER ILLUSTRATION: *I Can See Clearly Now,* by Sally Van Doren, 2020. Photograph by
Laszlo Gyorsok.

PAGE 71: *We Live Phonetically,* by Sally Van Doren, 2020. Photograph by Laszlo Gyorsok.

Grateful acknowledgment is made to the editors of the following publications, in which
the following poems first appeared: *Birmingham Poetry Review:* "Further up the Road";
Cornwall Chronicle: "Tomatoes and Peaches"; *Crazyhorse:* "Up Against It"; *december:*
"After Every There 3" and "Funk"; *Irises: The University of Canberra Vice-Chancellor's
International Poetry Prize* (anthology): "I Remember Telemachus"; *Kestrel:* "A to Z"
and "Tweak"; *Litchfield Magazine:* "Puzzle"; *Live Mag!:* "Palette" and "Scene"; *Poetry
Ireland Review:* "Double Entendre"; *Poetry London:* "Between the Bed and the Clock";
PoetryMagazine.com: "Stopping"; *Prairie Schooner:* "St. Patrick's Day"; and *2River View:*
"Domesticated" and "Mildred's Granddaughter."

LIBRARY OF CONGRESS CATALOGING-IN-PUBLICATION DATA

Names: Van Doren, Sally, author.
Title: Sibilance : poems / Sally Van Doren.
Description: Baton Rouge : Louisiana State University Press, [2023]
Identifiers: LCCN 2023004005 (print) | LCCN 2023004006 (ebook) |
    ISBN 978-0-8071-8018-1 (paperback) | ISBN 978-0-8071-8062-4 (pdf) |
    ISBN 978-0-8071-8061-7 (epub)
Subjects: LCGFT: Poetry.
Classification: LCC PS3622.A58548 S53 2023 (print) | LCC PS3622.A58548 (ebook) |
    DDC 811/.6—dc23/eng/20230206
LC record available at https://lccn.loc.gov/2023004005
LC ebook record available at https://lccn.loc.gov/2023004006

*for my husband
and our parents*

Contents

Sibilance

A TO Z

A baby carried all my genes
forward, high up in the
hierarchy of jurisprudence
but lower than the knowledge
of the quintessential eavesdropper,

way to the left of the excuse,
above the zero. That baby
loaded us up with his first words.
We listened to every letter. He
exhaled and we lost our lives.

I want to claim
that burst of blue,
to register it as an
antidote to the explosion
of too much emotion,
the yellows, reds, and greens
that bombard my morning
vision. Can we get
along or can't we?
Not when one young man
sets his anger on fire
and it's lights out
for everyone around him.

APOLITICAL

It is Wednesday
and I am trying to
ignore the many
intrusions on my
quiet morning. I
poached an egg
the color of his face
and ate it for breakfast.
We have found a
pastor in the field
who will minister
to our deepest needs.
We want someone to
smile and tell us where
to shop. Our bellies
sally forth from
under our tightened
belts. Give me a holy
consort, a mask to make
this moment in limbo
sacred . . . cricket, Weed-
wacker, FedEx truck.
The sunflowers tower
in their august glory
until the heft of their
seedy heads topples them.

BETWEEN THE BED
AND THE CLOCK

I'm personable. I play tennis
with aplomb. I can delineate
the distance from the net
to the baseline with a flick
of my new forehand. My
opponents are my friends
and I watch as they crawl
out of their beds, into
others', and back. A constant
give-and-take in this
flurry of stasis we call
a match. Light it and
see how the shellac
glimmers before it chars.
My spandex holds me tight
as I smolder in the rising
heat. Love and love.

BITTEN

You brought her to me
in a box on the subway
through Penn Station

past Rahway, Metuchen,
and all the other towns
whose names I never

attached to their locations.
She attached to me and
peed on my silk comforter

when I stayed out late.
A farm became her destination.
One gray, pissy pussy

who could never call
that I. M. Pei cinder block
home. One gift of yours

that adorns me no more,
no less than the diamond
you strung around my neck.

THE BODY POLITIC:
PRESS CONFERENCE

I'll admit I'm a
little tired because
we fooled around
a lot last night, up,
down, and all around
the body, the one
that had started
to doubt whether
or not it could
keep on going for it,
the one that thought
of giving up on getting
what it was afraid
to ask for. That body,
in the dark, soft night,
(or was it early morning?)
answered every question.

CELEBRITY SIGHTING

I take a walk in the park
most afternoons after lunch,
and yesterday, feeling a little blue
that our dog had died, our boys
had gone to college, and the house

where we raised them,
a modernist Midwestern nest
flanked by dogwoods and
three species of magnolia,
would soon be inhabited

by another family with younger
kids and a younger dog,
I was hoping I would run
into someone I knew in this city
newish to me as a slightly more

permanent, temporary roost, and
there they came, around the bend
in front of Turtle Pond, holding
hands, I think, or did I imagine
that fleet feint of the familiar?

CLEMENCY

She is very beautiful
without her shirt on,
standing in between the bed
and the bathroom. There
was a man with her
yesterday, but tonight she
is alone. She has gone
into the closet and all
I can see now is her
silhouette behind the frosted
glass door. I invited
her to accompany me
out over the rooftops.
She declined while
removing her left sock
and then her right.
But here, she said,
take my bare feet
and use them to show you
the way through the window.
I'll wait on the bed
until you have had your fill
of moonscape and skyscraper.
And then you can return
to me and reinvent me
once more, head to toe.

CONFERENCE

My relationship with
the dishwasher is private.
How dare you insert

your petty poetics
into my utensil rack.
I had a best friend once

and she knew the difference
between illness and love
only she forgot it every time

I walked into the room.
When I look at you
I see assonance and taste

abstinence. My father
appears young and handsome.
Haven't we heard these

repetitions before? It doesn't
matter. I have used my own
words this time. Try them.

CURSIVE

The sky is short today
and wide in the face.
I look down to avoid

its disapproval. The dirt
floor looks back at me.
I'm in the basement,

a legitimate scapegoat
squatting on a ballpoint pen,
watching the red ink spread.

DAUGHTER

We're talking about learning
that our mother's mind
has wandered way off course
and all this time I have been

following it, buying her diapers,
paying her bills, calling her
every day, watering her cactus.
She's been pricked by the thorn

of decay. Her voice gets more
shrill with each advance. I'm
afraid to put myself in her head,
perched in a heightened state

I can't access. Last month she
called to say "Happy Birthday"
and it sent me soaring, even when
I found out that my younger brother

had put her up to it. I knew what she
once knew and now neither of us do.
Yesterday she told me she was out
of fish oil. I add it to the list.

DEATH OF AN IMPLEMENT

She was used to hearing
from the alarm and her phone,
but when her pen fell off

the bedside table and yelled "ouch!"
it startled her. She looked at it
lying on the beige, low-pile,

wall-to-wall carpeting and asked,
"Are you okay?" but it did not reply,
nor would it ever speak again.

She picked it up, shook it, and
held it to her ear, then used it
until it ran out, some thirty days later.

DERMATOGRAPHIC

Today is Wednesday
and I'm conditioned
to bawl at ten a.m.

I exposed my midriff
for fifty-seven years to get
news coverage. Scrape

my belly skin to see
if your handwriting
appears there. Together

we will read what you
have done and why it
pains you. Just under

my navel it says you
deprived me of a lifetime
of fertility. I rub up

against you each night
while we sweat to release
the poems I never painted.

DESSERT

As the busboy seized
our parfait glasses
we fixated on the pittance

of cream left
on our violet tablecloth.
Is our mood

adjustable? The omniscient
bust in the alcove
stimulates a profusion of

aspirations. I want
more than you do and
I intend to get it.

DO IT

Because she was loathe
to write the same poem
over and over again,

the spinstress memorized
obscure tracts of scientific
data and used that diction

instead of the same old,
same old soundtrack
running through her mind.

Zeatin and gliadin
replaced hunger and thirst.
Longing no longer appeared

on the radar. She slapped
her own hand every time
it reached for satisfaction.

Clipped to the pinions
emitted from her dendrites,
she relied on axons to

deliver her from stasis.
So she could finally, fabulously
FUCK THE FLUX.

DOMESTICATED

I left Black Creek to come
here to distance myself
from the magnolia leaves
pressing themselves against
my south-facing windows. I
sought to distinguish myself,
the self desperate for the
dithyramb, the self opening
and closing the door to the cellar
in my dollhouse on wheels.
My mother had painted the doors
blue and the stucco walls yellow.
I was not inclined to flock
to the forever she followed,
but I brought her flowers
yesterday, yellow daffodils
to fill her crystal vases.

DOUBLE ENTENDRE

I'd really like to reveal
myself to you, but I am
prevented from doing so
by my frenum, the muscle
between my two front teeth
that acts as a bodyguard
whenever I turn my sights
inward to dispel the lethargy
swarming around the analyst
in me who doesn't want to look
under my tongue. Would
you either? I'm finally alone
in my quiet mouth. Let's make
a pact. If I don't unearth
my weaknesses, then I won't
bury you with them. I'll spend
all night gargling with warm
salt water to practice. Then,
in the morning, we'll put our
fingers down our throats
and see who wins.

ECLOGUE

I found a fly at the bottom
of a sheet of paper in my
notebook. It lies there like
one of Emily Dickinson's
dried flowers, only I didn't
kill it. Upon closer inspection,

I realize it's a mosquito,
not a fly, and I know it was
coming for me, but somehow
went instead for the last line
I had written on the page
that day. Parts of its guts

are splayed on the opposing
page. I could flick them off
with my fingernail if I had
the nerve to touch them.
Flatten me in a book when
it's time to go and make it quick.

FUNK

We have the wherewithal
to weather this partial
eclipse, this moment
when the moon is
mottled, when the sun
thinks it doesn't want
to shine anymore.
The illuminations on your cheek
revive me. They are
disproportionate to
the lunar depressions,
they light up the relics
we keep in the basement
to remind us of how
much an ounce of faith
weighs. We measure
what we believe in by
cauterizing our leaking
windpipes. Mine are
dense with blisters. I'm
wholly fixated on
swallowing a new language:
words I can feel, sounds
I can emulate.

FURTHER UP THE ROAD

I won't write another word
until you minimize the time
we spend coveting each other's

shortcomings. I missed
the meeting where they
plotted out the trajectory

from nowhere to somewhere.
This pothole looks bigger
in June when the sun expands

it beyond its frame. I had
fallen in one limb at a time.
At midnight, you grabbed my rib

and flipped me over, earning us
both enough points to apply
for a promotion to morning.

GONE

I will look for the key
when you stop talking
about the time you
jumped off the eighteenth floor
of the parking garage
and landed on my
thirtieth birthday cake,
crushing the figurine
my mother had placed
there to represent
my iconic permanence.
I will never forgive
you for leaving the car
in reverse because I
unintentionally backed into
a space reserved for
maternity patients and
ran over the foot of a
nine-months-pregnant woman.
Did you fall or did you
jump? I have stapled
your black patent loafers
to this sheet of paper.
I don't think I want to
know your answer any
more. I felt your big toe
wedged against my ankle
last night and I stepped
on the gas. We drove the
car right off the Madison
Avenue Bridge together.

HOME

I know the back roads here.
They lead the way, this
loop within the loop
of my each and every day.

I won't belabor you
with yammer and yarn.
Just hold up the stars while
I convince you to stay.

ICE STORM

It was really good that school
was called off today because
we didn't have to get up to
get the boys up. I just dozed
from 6:52 until about eight,
drifting in and out of a post-
orgasmic haze. When I went
into the kitchen I noticed that
a few of the magnolia branches
had snapped from the weight
of the ice, but a dry crunch coated
the driveway and I did not slip
on my way to get the newspapers. Nice
to start a winter morning with infinity.

I REMEMBER TELEMACHUS

I am susceptible to
forgetfulness. I know
where my car keys are
now, submissively tied
to the whistle I have
never blown in self-defense,
but I can't recall the conversation
you say we had about whether
or not our friends had mentioned
that they would like to meet us
in Portugal next fall. Some things
I let lapse, like most of my
college experience, but I'm
a pushover for lavender and
open magnolia blossoms. I'm
better at sight than recording
words, but if I could harness
the sound of your voice
when you're happy, like it was
last night when we arrived late
at the party on the lake because
the afternoon light detained us,
I would change my ways.

JUNE DISORIENT

Quick, dismantle the
petals spreading from
the center of the peony.

If we bisect the pistil, we
won't have to open the door
and let everyone else in.

JVD

The key to understanding me
lies undetected on the top
shelf of my grandfather's
work bench. He never knew
me because he died not long after
my father married my mother
in her parents' living room.
He was gassed in the trenches
in France at eighteen, and though
he survived, he was often sick.
He came down the stairs from his bed
to give her away. My mother carried
his work bench from the basement
of the house on Edgewood Drive
to the basement of our house
on Black Creek Lane where I stood
by the bench to spy on my nineteen-
year-old brother and his girlfriend
by the pool in the backyard. Wooden
and worn, it was rarely used, except
as a table for my brothers' molds
and supplies for their lead soldiers.
My middle brother burned his hand
pouring the hot grey melt into the shape
of an army man with a gun.
We kept the figurines in a shoe box
under the bench, miniature mannequins
awaiting the fight, inanimate, heavy,
their rifles poised.

KINDLING

Just when I thought
I knew what to do
to keep myself from
thinking, I felt a
feeling that made

me forget the years
of trying to rub
two sticks together
to make fire. I felt
the fire between

the two sticks. If I
knew how not to put
it out, I would do that
forever and fuel
myself on its flicker.

LOPSIDED

She's an infirm hipster
handicapped by an eerie
hankering for the negative
even when a jocular
positive cruises up her
driveway in a tank. She
might throw him a
brochure from her balcony,
but that's the only spatial
recognition he will get
this week, when, buried
under a spontaneous
blow-dry bar, she can't be
excavated from her insomnia.
It was a book that pushed
her off the edge, and now
all she can do is jot down
one vehement letter after
another to make a bolster
for her wobbly head. See
that dazed bulldozer? It's
been sent to trample her
unhinged reminiscence.
Everything's on the downside
except for her bangs, which are
flipping out and up like those of a '70s
sitcom housewife which she
will never be. It's too late
for that. Every constructed
word makes an eyeshade which
shields her from the burgeoning
Second Avenue subway. You and
I are invited to malinger in her
nightmares as long as we don't talk.

MADELEINE

There was a period of time, once our boys had grown, when the eggs which had faithfully created them started to fail, and the bloody membranes I could count upon to color the water of my toilet once a month began to diminish, at first haltingly, for a few weeks perhaps, and then for several months, until finally a full year elapsed with no clumps of red pigment extruding from my uterus.

The waxing reluctance of their appearance coincided with fluctuating ranges of temperature and humidity within their larger host, which stretched from my internal organs to the surface of my skin. I awoke from housewifely lassitude in the pre-dawn dark, just before the swallows set upon the fields, to a wetness coursing through my torso, uninhibited by my loose nightgown and the soft cotton sheets impinging upon the liquid's escape.

Although I would come to expect the heat that gathered while I slept and did not announce itself fully until the tepid pool collecting in the small of my back sent a message up my spine to the drenched nape of my neck that I must open my eyes, bringing an abrupt end to the safety of sleep so that I wouldn't drown in the pressure cooker I had become, I was unaccustomed to being awake at that hour next to the quiet body of my resting husband.

I did not wish to impede upon his hiatus from wakefulness any more than my throwing off of our silk coverlet late in the night may have done, nor did I dare touch him with my scarlet fingers or toes. During this swelling expanse of minutes, I thought, more than once, that words would save me, and I came up with phrases I could memorize through repetition and imprint upon my early-morning mind so that they would be guaranteed to be recollected later on when I wrote in my journal. But it was painting that was my secret friend. Lying there, waiting to cool off, waiting for the bedsheets to dry, I imagined applying yellow ochre, raw umber, and burnt sienna to a stretched linen canvas. In this way, I prepared myself to meet the master ripening within me.

MASQUERADE

I have lost
all perspective.
Will my friend

live or die?
Do we have
all we have

ever wanted
or are we
about to have

nothing? Fine,
put your mask
on and don't

answer my questions.
You are beautiful
in your denial.

MILDRED'S
GRANDDAUGHTER

This is a poem about
a woman who lived
forever. She lived through
years of poetry readings.
She lived through many
presidencies. She
lived through the births
of her sons and
grandsons. She never
stopped for death
and ate when and
whatever she wanted.
She lost track of
time sometimes,
but it never caught
up to her. The motivating
principle of her life
resembled a mass of
wisteria levitating
over the house next
door. The neighbors
invited her in and
offered her tea
in every season.
She drank it to
warm her heart,
to flush out the
memories of those
who would not love her.

MWAH

Muscle your way into
the mutant harness
which holds back all

the haywire histamines
surging to my skin's
surface. The itching's

autonomous. A moist,
cool lip compress
is what they prescribe.

This scribe sees red
ink on purple veins.
Fingernails aweigh. We

want soft, not brittle.
That metal bit grates
against tender gums.

Each yank turns my chin
in a new direction.
The tongue's fascia runs

helter-skelter for shelter.
Would you decamp
with me to an omen-free

mouth? I drool over
your brightened teeth
for a taste of ecstatic

saliva. Open wide, portal,
my avatar and I are
breaking out of the stall.

NURSERY

The sun sealed the snowfield
like epoxy—not one daffodil
could pierce it to announce
that April was a week away.
We remained frozen under
the conjecture that no coming
warm breeze could flush away
the ice in our lungs. But our eye
could see green even if it did
not yet exist. We smudged a daub
of that cold lacquer in each
of our nostrils until we were high
on the whenever. We detached our
beard and hung it discreetly next to
the bucket collecting syrup from
the maple. We sought a clear flow,
a sheath to douse our roots in,
proof that in the substratum
of our index finger, blood and oxygen
mixed and gave rise to a mutant foetus
sucking at the paps of the first
word that refused to darken the page.

ORNAMENT

The moon pulled her skirt
up and I saw my aptitude
underneath it before
she crossed her legs.
In a puff of moisture
my future morphed
from a seed bed to a siesta.
No sound, just a loosened
girdle orbiting the home
planet. I estimate a thousand
or so revolutions before
we get to look up again
and see her lighting the way.

PALETTE

Blue is not forgotten.
Red reigns next to it,
conquering yellow which
quivers under the bench

in the waiting room, hiding
from the consequence of
green. Forgive me for being
gray. I don't understand

the nature of color. I paint
myself with stripes to clarify
my intentions. Every once
in a while, orange bleeds

from the tip of my pen
into my pupil and my purple
eye sees the sun running
to the end of the world.

PATIENCE

I went to Walgreens yesterday,
after dropping my husband
at the airport, and bought
the only shower bench with arms
they had. It cost $69.99.
I took it to my mother's
apartment, pulled the four legs,
two arms, seat, and back
out of the box and assembled it
without tools, as advertised.

There was a moment of doubt
when I wasn't sure I could
cram the aluminum leg into
the corresponding socket
because of the plastic teeth lining
the inner tube, but I found
by applying pressure and
twisting the leg as I pushed,
it would slide in.

I took a photo of my handiwork
on my phone, then walked down
one floor through five corridors
and three sets of automatic doors
to the Extended Care Unit
where my ninety-year-old stepdad
was hanging like a baby
from the stork's mouth
in a net attached to a small crane
used to move patients like him
who are immobilized, in his case,
by a brace around his left hip

(which was replaced with
titanium years ago, and
"revised" in an eight-hour
surgery last month).

Four nurse aides had plucked
him from his recliner and now
lowered him onto his bed
for his post-PT nap.
My mother reclined
in the recliner next to his.
I showed her the photo
of her new shower chair and
she clapped her hands.
As they both nodded off,
I found the brown puzzle piece
with a jagged green tip and, with
a bit of jiggling, put it in its place.

PEN PAL

This pen is a little
on the slim side,
best suited to live
in a purse, pulled
out on occasion
to jot down a note
or sign a check, without
adding any more heft
to an already over-
burdened left shoulder.
It's from the hotel
where we stayed a few
years ago to watch Sam
play football or from
the one in DC near
his apartment. How it
travels with me through
this path of mother to
son, lightly, pointedly,
with a purpose.

PHANTOM

My hand has run into my heart.
Here, feel how my fingers
furnish my lungs. I am not
intimidated by the groping

thumb. I let it plumb the last
place I have gone to hide.
If you follow me, I will cut
down the Linden tree under

which you were born.
Remember that I was there
at your beginning. I produced

you. I will prune your limbs
if I need to. Let's rest here
in the dark before you disappear.

PONTOON

I am old enough now
to recognize the fjord
that plummets down

between my breasts,
over my belly, and
onto the sandbar

of my pubic bone.
When you signed up
for this body, water

surrounded it. We
pummel my tendons
to release the fluid

and I swallow fish oil
to retain it. If you touch
me in the night your

finger burns. My sweat
leaks, my hands swell,
my soft tissues fray.

A measuring cup can't
hold my ingredients,
but I don't yet shatter.

We bob along in awe
of our surroundings, soaking
the sheets, sleeping on

the fly, eyes askew, lashes
drenched, until that last egg
dries up and floats away.

PRANK

The amphibians were crabby.
They crawled up on top
of the rocks and sunned
themselves under the shade

of the penumbra tree. They
shaved the cutesy webbing
off their feet, became ambulatory,
and walked upright out of the swamp

and into our living room. My husband
speared them with the fire poker. He
stuck them in the wood stove, where
they roasted to a crisp. He dipped

them in chocolate and fed them
to our guests for dessert.

PUZZLE

The rain encroaches
upon this alert chance
to distinguish water
from air. If we jimmy

the window latch,
the screen comes closer
to separating us from
the vector at the end

of May, the end of a time
when we knew what
to expect from summer.
We hear the rain and we

remember how the blue sky
arrived from wherever it came.

QUADRANT

I need to make room for the table
and the chair and the green and gold
tapestry. I don't need to accommodate
your directions to contradict myself.

I do that regularly enough
all on my own. Can you see
the seascape above the tan leather
chair? It's iconic. Once we

dilated our third eye just for fun
and the red pigment in the square
hanging next to the window
bludgeoned us with its bright stare.

I never wanted to pick my hand
up off the frame. I left it
there to pacify the vertical
equilibrium assaulting my

bloody ego. There was a scuffle
over who was ahead and who
was behind. Never you mind,
we nailed it right there, line by line.

RECLAMATION

It was the first day of summer.
We had sweat on the tennis court.
The hay was high in the fields.

I was high on Corona Light,
you were washing the lettuce.
There were many possible

distractions: the turkeys
nesting in the blueberries,
the groundhogs waddling

from the barn to the garage,
the bluebirds flying from
the corncrib to the woodshed.

Your dad had died a month
before. My mom couldn't
remember my name.

RESOLUTION

The parliament convenes
at four a.m. The liberals tell
my temporal lobe to loosen up.

The conservatives shriek at me
to count the coins dropping
from the change machine.

One paper dollar can convert
to all sorts of things, but I've
quarantined mine in a catalogue

of can't haves. I'd like my art to
breathe and take form and my body
to absolve itself of lust.

ST. PATRICK'S DAY

I've been dreaming about the dead
lately, one old friend long dead
and another old friend only dead
to me through lack of recent

communication. Dad's birthday
is coming up and I wonder how
he will welcome Mom. (At ninety, she
will soon celebrate her tenth wedding

anniversary with his college roommate.)
My guess is they will be glad to see
each other and he will hold no
grudge against her for holding

onto his old friend. I like to imagine
him giving her a hug that will melt
away her present knee and shoulder
pains. All aches gone. All debts forgiven.

SCENE

The impending light
pushes out from
an unstable center.

It tries to convert
flux into stasis. I
watch it from my

indolent perch
on the couch. If it
pushes too hard

we will capsize.
I prefer to regard
it from across

the room, letting
it guide me without
burning a hole in my sight.

SÉANCE

I will invite you over to spend
the night with me and seven
other girls. We'll play leapfrog
first in the front hall then
aggravate my mother by yanking
all the slipcovers off the living room
sofas and draping them over
the credenza in the dining room
to make an entrance to our fort.
There's no harm in depositing
our dreams in our fingertips. You
lie down in the middle of our circle.
We count to ten and there, with
our eyes closed at the edge
of the area rug, two fingers per
ten-year-old girl, we lift you up,
and, when we realize you are floating,
we shriek and you drop, butt to the
carpet, head to the hardwood floor.

SECOND AVENUE

The narcissist in me
is pushing hard against

the brick walls that line
the streets of this city.

I have rubbed my hands
raw trying to climb

their mortar. But look,
underneath the manicured

tips lie pearly half-moons
unscarred by effort. This

finger points at you. Fair
warning for the next time

you use me to make
yourself feel worse.

SIBILANCE

I'm stuck seeking out
the one sound that will
astonish me, you, us, them,
whoever lurks around the corner
whispering sweet somethings
to the stalwart audience,
the stifled ears that now

hear shapes and sights
they never thought would
sidle over from their circle
to slum in our circumference,
hissing and spitting, one radius
pitted against another, until
the *s* curve enters, symbolizing

osmosis, searing itself to our half-
smile. It's a sign on our skin
designed to synthesize the serifs
rushing in to capsize the ocean-
going vessel of our souls.
A scream, a sigh, an estimate
of what it takes to pass from

one state to another, to simulate
transformation, to embrace
the staccato on the slate roof
surging down the sewer pipes,
surrounding our sense of self
with the senses of all other selves,
fusing us onto the shoulders of the sun.

SIDEARM SONNET

The trees on this
side of Route 7
straighten up when
the passing trucks
spray their roots
with slush. They
call an audible,
throwing snow
onto the roof tops
of the minivans
and Chevy Novas.
We're not waiting
around to hear where
you're going without us.

SOCIAL CONSTRUCT

This quiet fifth-floor corner,
mid-block, muffles the sirens,
horns, and buses of the busy
avenues, but mornings, there's

the *peck, peck, peck* of the
hammer of the man building
the new high-rise to the east,
not high enough yet to block

our view of the sun's rise. How
does he do it, one arm-raise
at a time, one I beam wedged
into another. The cement trucks

below and the cranes above frame
him as he pounds into the day.

SOMETIMES AND ALWAYS

And all this time
it was the leaves,
not the trees, yelling
at us to catch hold
of the coyote's tail
and use it to brush
the hair out of our eyes
so we could see
the voluptuous difference
between reticence and
a wide-open lens.
Had we not shrunk
from its patchy coat
when it leapt from its
sun nap in the field,
we might have seen
the color of its heart,
the one that beats like
ours, without hearing
autumn come, the one
that knows how to
serenade the last people
who will love us.

SORRY

I'm of too many minds today,
the grade-school girl in spasms
over finding a secure place
to clamp her self-portrait,
charcoal lines now defining

her jowl as the years
since then have magnified
to a near continent of a lifetime.
We're on the rocks on the South Pole,
wetter than we're supposed to be,

our sonic valves bursting with steam
meant to tilt the world to its other
axis. Molecules no longer matter.
We need to regulate the internal slop
that heats the whole planet, we're

scalding hot without a winter,
without the magnet that melds us
to the magma. Sweatier than that
bawling baby born this morning.
She's got everything to cry for.

STAND-UP POET

I'm here because I can't
take one more poetry reading.
Raise your hand if you have
ever been to one. As I suspected,
not many people would willingly
submit themselves to an hour-long
lyric discourse on loneliness and death.

Even a two-drink minimum does little
to make the stream bubble happily
over the rocks. We're like the stagnant
brown water that puddles in the mud
between the algae-covered concrete
sewer posts in a Missouri creek.
Even the tadpoles take a pass.

Once, we told a joke in the middle
of a poem only to be reprimanded
later for misstating the punch line.
Our gift is not gab. Our toupee
doesn't gleam under the hot, bright
stage lights. We sit in the corner
and sip a Bud Light, laughing when
the pretty young mother in the wool
cap mentions that not shaving
her pubic hair is a benefit of marriage,
crying when we feel the tender follicles
ripped from their fertile fonts.

STATIONERY

I don't have what I need
most of the time now,

so I'm looking for new
needs. I left those important

numbers in a book
that I left in the place

I'm going to this afternoon,
but I needed them last night

when I didn't have them.
There are many other papers

that fall prey to this escapade
of escapism we are presently

on the periphery of. You can
interrogate me all you want,

but the only citation you
can plaster on my front door

is the one that says, "No one
is home." I will ask you

one more time, less forcibly
this time, but no less urgently,

to ignore the piles of snow
and come appropriate me.

I'll stay stuck in this slush
until then. It's the only way

I know how to emanate
on a clean, dry sheet.

STOPPING

Not starting. A certain
level of discomfort

should be expected.
You think you can cut

me out of your life but
our aperture never closed.

You can bandy about in
your underpants all you want

but I know where you sit
and I know where we stand.

SUN AND MOON IN LIBRA

I believed what the psychic
told me seven years ago
and two parts of it have
come true: one having to do
with tears, the other,
Pennsylvania. I'd like to
choreograph the rest of my
tomorrows, but I hear only
the music which tells me
I'm dreaming in the past.
At least I'm prepared for
the next day that doesn't come.
On this sunny morning, the present
and I dismantle the black-eyed
Susan, petal by petal, taking
what nature gave us and lining
it up on the windowsill. Sneezing
occasionally, we say "Bless you,"
wipe our noses, and soldier on.

TOEHOLD

It's there, wedged into
the crawlspace between
the lung and the ribcage,
stuck like a corn kernel

in a notch with a vantage
point of my one kidney.
It's jostled by my gasps,
disoriented by my laugh,

but it's the tarmac I land
and take off from. Is the
soul rooted to the heart?
I'll vouch for the eye that

can't see, the censored
jaw, the tangled skeleton.
I've got bones and blood
and breath riding on this.

TOMATOES AND PEACHES

I can't think of any other words besides
happy and *peaceful* to describe this moment.

I'll use this August morning as sustenance
when *sad* and *stressed* become the norm.

The words that elude me are legible
on the raindrops on the maple leaves,

on the line of pine trees on the ridge
of Yelping Hill, and, just beyond them,

on the pale-blue and white pages
of sky and cloud hovering above the Hollow.

TRANSVERSAL

I'm too straightforward so
the wings of this plane and
I will lead you to my bedroom

where my husband folds the silk
comforter and places it at the foot
of our bed in my absence. It should

feel abnormal to land beside the river,
but its flood plains are always home.
I'm never alone in the confluence.

TWEAK

It feels like so long
since I have mentioned
myself in our conversations
that I must reintroduce
you to my latest incarnation.

Gone are the squiggles
and the interlocutions.
I only yell and sleep.
Two modes that prepare me
for marriage and motherhood.

See the picture of me
on the refrigerator? I took that
when I knew what kind of
woman I could be. You can bob
your head all you want to,

but I'm not acknowledging you
anymore. I want to harness
the torpedo in my chest
and follow it to a curvilinear
conclusion. Just a necessary

adjustment to this plush portrait.
Beauty arrives when it is
sick and tired of waiting,
when it no longer hears
the beat of the bass drum.

UNDERSTUDY

She's not who I
thought she was
and I no longer
recognize the face
that wakes me up
in the mirror each
morning. We're a
set of twins with
behavioral tics that
link us to defunct
pensions. We're
not looking at you
to define us. We're
looking away from you,
so stop coming into
the bathroom and asking
questions. We have
no answers. We decorate
our features daily to form
new acronyms. Go ahead,
try to name us. We have
encoded our inventories
to prevent identity theft.
What would we give you
for free? Anonymity.

UP AGAINST IT

We will foist ourselves
on the bare branches
of the viburnum like
a frozen page of grocery
coupons, our polish
wearing off under the
fickle December sun,
gone again, come again,
leaving us to juggle for
light when the low clouds
gloss over our imperfections.
I once poured enamel
on my eyelashes to
emblazon this Berkshire
vista, but the leafless woods
hold promise just out
of reach. We listen as
the words fall in chunks
of ice from the metal roof.

VISITATION

Does one death prepare
you for another? I'm not
looking forward to losing
my mother, or the others
I hold dear. I watch
those losing theirs and
remember what it was like.
Different every death? I
hope so. That center of sobs
and separation overlaps and
spreads into circles I have
reserved for the living.

Whether breath is taken
with pain or confusion,
it's still attached to warm
flesh and the pulse of a mind
inclined to connect to
our network of family
and friends, our constellation
in a universe designed
to define us. This benign
guide we follow. We
bind ourselves closer to
prevent dispersal. We
save our cries for another
day, another body.

WITNESS

I saw what you did
but I am not at liberty
to tell anyone about it.
Anyone is not predisposed

to hear the confessions
of the rat, the fink who
lets it fly in the face
of conventional decorum.

What you did to him
was not nearly as bad as
what she did to me.
Let's play a trick on the

upholders of fraternal
hygiene. I'll wash your
hands of it if you take
my fingerprints and

plaster them to the roof
of the moon. In its full
light, we can begin to read
the handwriting on the ceiling.

XENOPHILIA

l like our idyll,
eye on cheek,
tongue on teeth,
peach juice in
prosecco, no
other hands
or mouths
pressing on
our privacy.
The balcony
overlooks the
garden where
the gardenias
climb up and
over the trellis,
their sweet sight
and taste spreading
through this June
afternoon, peaking
in this room with
a single view, this
bed for two.

YOU TELL ME

I haven't told the truth
in so long that you
can't blame me
for not knowing

the difference between
pain and pleasure.
I've tricked myself
into believing in

the intermittent raindrops
separating my window
from the fire escape
on the building across from me.

Is that water or are those streaks
of dirt clouding my view?
If you join me on the ledge
you will find, as I have,

that there is security
in the fusion of liquid and
matter. *What does it matter?*
we are prompted to ask.

ZIGZAG

Most mornings I rearrange
flowers, putting *a* next to *b*,
snipping off the head of a wilted *c*.

When the tip of *d* careens to the left,
it joins the other dead and dented petals
in the straw basket in the mudroom sink,

the contents of which will be tossed
into the hayfield where the clover and
alfalfa will camouflage their decay.

Afternoons, I circle back to pen and ink,
scrutinize the width and depth of an arc,
sharpen charcoal to a carved point, and

wing a blue pencil around an imagined radius,
creating areas off-limits to the diameters
of passersby. Should you like me

to spell it out for you, it is in these marks
and ways that I mark the days, these days
being ones that resist circumscription.

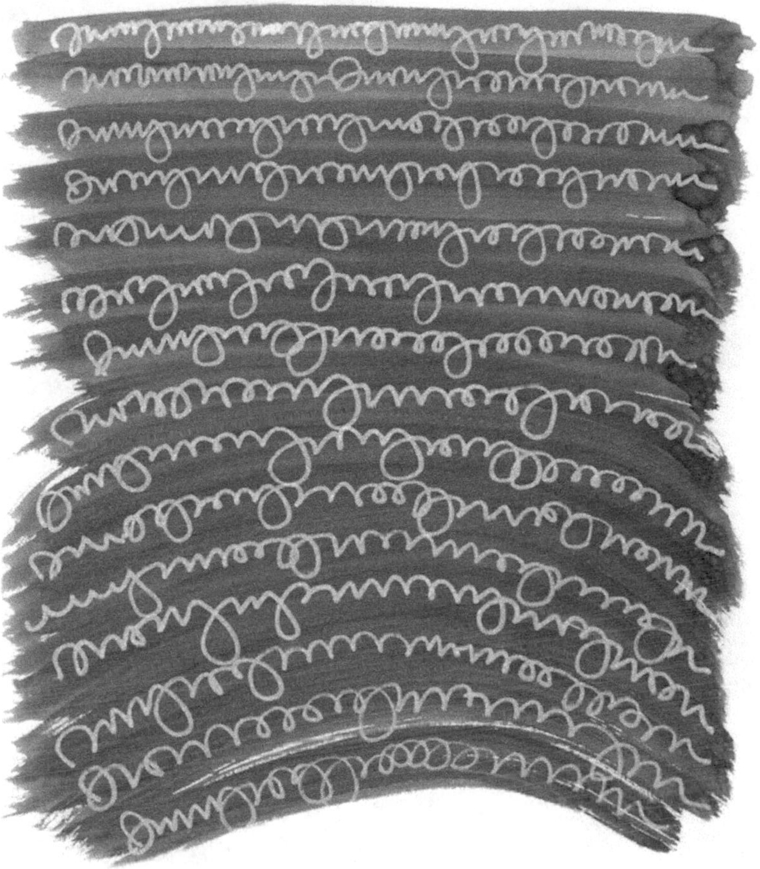

Notes

"After Every There 3" is inspired by a watercolor of the same title by Eva Lundsager.

The title "Between the Bed and the Clock" is a play on *Between the Clock and the Bed*, the title of paintings by Edvard Munch and Jasper Johns.

The line "foetus / sucking at the paps" in "Nursery" owes a debt to a phrase in Sylvia Plath's poem "The Stones."

"Scene" is after TM Davy's painting *Candela* (*Afterimage Golden*).

The title "Sometimes and Always" is taken from the last line of John Ashbery's poem "At North Farm."

Printed in the USA
CPSIA information can be obtained
at www.ICGtesting.com
LVHW090819041223
765473LV00004B/696